I Can Listen to English! 3

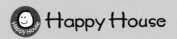

Dear Teachers and Parents,

Welcome to Happy House "I Can Listen to English!"

Happy House Listening is designed to meet the needs and interests of children. It aims to help children develop and improve the listening skills necessary to communicate in a fun environment. The full-color illustrations are based on a creative storyline that includes funny characters like Toby and Cory, elves who live in the attic. The fantastic story encourages children to build their English listening skills. Happy House Listening is a three-level course containing 10 units, and after every five units, four-page reviews for each level. Each unit features a question and an answer with 8~10 alternative words. A topic which draws on the everyday lives and experiences of children with a fun story has been added. This book is child-centered in order to benefit young children and to prepare them for the fruitful use of English listening at a higher level.

• E2K Contents

A creative group that provides quality contents and educational services in English for ESL and EFL students.
The goal of E2K is to make the finest quality materials to make learning English more enjoyable for students.

TABLE OF CONTENTS

HOW TO USE
"I CAN LISTEN TO ENGLISH!"

Chant Listening

It helps to present new structures and new words in a fun and easy way. And it also provides motivation for listening.

Sentence Listening

This listening exercise reinforces the previous pages to help students learn sentence structures.

Word Listening

This listening exercise provides thorough practice in using new words.

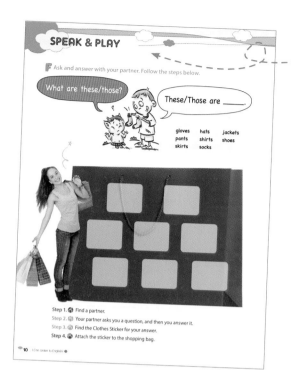

Speak & Play

This oral activity encourages communication by playing a game.

Writing

These listening activities give learners the opportunity to practice structures and words by writing.

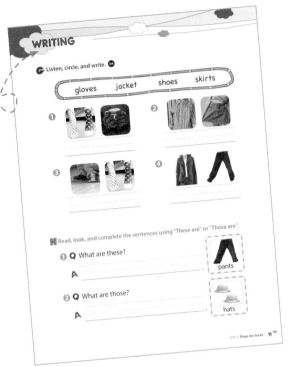

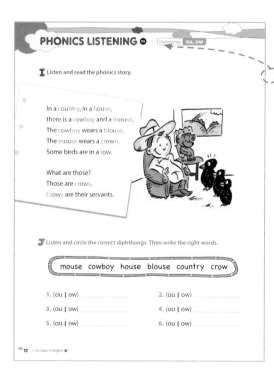

Phonics Listening

This phonics story gives learners the chance to read short stories. This listening and writing activity contains questions designed to improve students' understanding of phonics rules.

Review

These are systematic recycling and review pages.

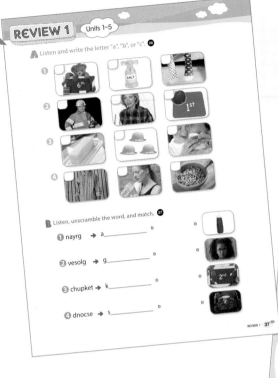

Phonics Review

The various questions in this section help learners to understand phonics rules and improve their listening, reading, and writing skills. They also help increase learners' vocabularies.

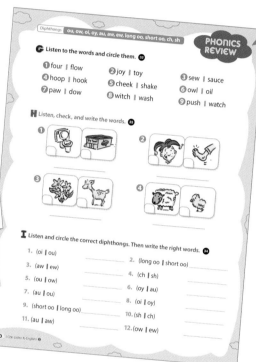

UNIT 01

These Are Socks

CHANT LISTENING 01

A Listen and chant.
Then circle the clothes you hear in the chant.

B Listen, write the number, and match.

pants   jacket   shirt   gloves

C Listen, look, and circle.

1    shirts   (skirts)   shoes

2    socks   shoes   skirts

3    skirts   jackets   shoes

4    hats   socks   pants

D Listen, check, and match.

1. ○   ○ Those are shirts.

2. ○   ○ These are socks.

3. ○   ○ These are gloves.

4. ○   ○ Those are hats.

E Listen, look, and circle "a" or "b".

SPEAK & PLAY

F Ask and answer with your partner. Follow the steps below.

What are these/those?

These/Those are _____.

gloves	hats	jackets
pants	shirts	shoes
skirts	socks	

Step 1. Find a partner.

Step 2. Your partner asks you a question, and then you answer it.

Step 3. Find the Clothes Sticker for your answer.

Step 4. Attach the sticker to the shopping bag.

WRITING

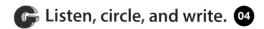

🎧 Listen, circle, and write. **04**

> gloves   jacket   shoes   skirts

❶ _____

❷ _____

❸ _____

❹ _____

H Read, look, and complete the sentences using "These are" or "Those are".

❶ **Q** What are these?

A _____
_____ .

pants

❷ **Q** What are those?

A _____
_____ .

hats

I Listen and read the phonics story.

In a country, in a house,
there is a cowboy and a mouse.
The cowboy wears a blouse.
The mouse wears a crown.
Some birds are in a row.

What are those?
Those are crows.
Crows are their servants.

J Listen and circle the correct diphthongs. Then write the right words.

> mouse   cowboy   house   blouse   country   crow

1. (ou | ow) _____
2. (ou | ow) _____
3. (ou | ow) _____
4. (ou | ow) _____
5. (ou | ow) _____
6. (ou | ow) _____

UNIT 02

I'm in the First Grade

 A Listen and chant.
Then circle the ordinal numbers you hear in the chant.

B Listen, circle, and match.

 ○ ○ third

 ○ ○ seventh

 ○ ○ fifth

 ○ ○ first

C Listen, check, and circle the word.

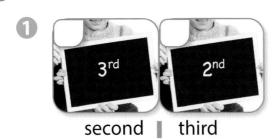

1 second | third

2 fifth | sixth

3 seventh | eighth

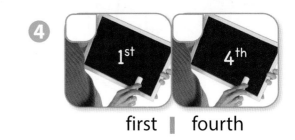

4 first | fourth

SENTENCE LISTENING ⓞ⑧

D Listen, check, and match.

1. ○ ○ I'm in the fourth grade.

2. ○ ○ I'm in the sixth grade.

3. ○ ○ I'm in the fifth grade.

4. ○ ○ I'm in the second grade.

E Listen, look, and circle "a" or "b".

SPEAK & PLAY

F Ask and answer with your partner. Follow the steps below.

What grade are you in?

I'm in the _____ grade.

| first | second | third | four |
| fifth | sixth | seventh | eight |

Step 1. Find eight partners who are in the different grades. Then write their names in the chalkboards.

Step 2. You ask your partners a question, and then they answer it.

Step 3. Find the Word Sticker for their answer.

Step 4. Attach the sticker to the chalkboard.

WRITING

G Listen, circle, and write. 🔟09

> fifth   first   second   third

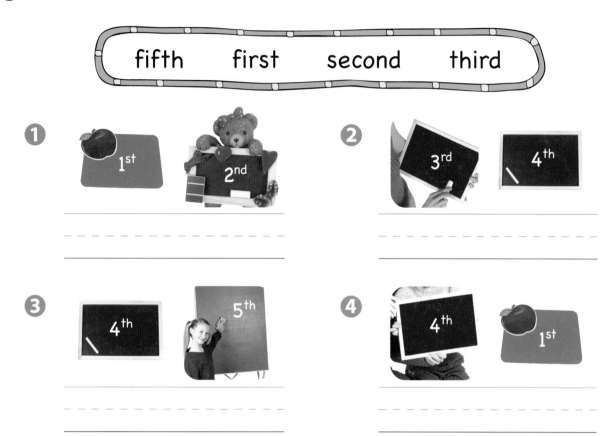

①

②

③

④

H Read, look, and complete the sentences using "in the ~ grade".

① **Q** What grade are you in?

   A I'm _____ .

7th

seventh

② **Q** What grade are you in?

   A I'm _____ .

3rd

third

Diphthongs **oi, oy**

I Listen and read the phonics story.

In Joy Toyshop,
a boy points at the yo-yo.
He gives some coins.

What grade are you in?
I'm in the second grade.

I see!
Here's your toy.
I want this oil truck, too!

J Listen and write the correct diphthongs and a word.

> toy   coin   oil   boy   point   toilet

1. _____ ⊕ l ⊜ _____   2. t ⊕ _____ ⊜ _____

3. b ⊕ ____ ⊜ _____   4. c ⊕ ____ ⊕ n ⊜ _____

5. t ⊕ ____ ⊕ let ⊜ _____   6. p ⊕ _____ ⊕ nt ⊜ _____

I'm Happy

CHANT LISTENING 11

A Listen and chant.
Then circle the faces expressing the feeling you hear in the chant.

B Listen, write the number, and match.

angry　　hungry　　cold　　sleepy

C Listen, look, and circle.

1  　　sad　　hot　　happy

2  　　thirsty　　sad　　happy

3  　　cold　　thirsty　　angry

4  　　hot　　sleepy　　cold

SENTENCE LISTENING 🔞

D Listen, check, and match.

① ○   ○ Are you sleepy?

② ○   ○ Are you hungry?

③ ○   ○ Is he thirsty?

④ ○   ○ Is he angry?

E Listen, look, and circle "a" or "b".

① a / b ② a / b ③ a / b

④ a / b ⑤ a / b ⑥ a / b

SPEAK & PLAY

F Ask and answer with your partner. Follow the steps below.

> Is he/she _____?

> Yes, he/she is. No, he/she isn't. He/She's _____.

happy	sad	angry	sleepy
hot	cold	hungry	thirsty

Step 1. Find eight partners.

Step 2. You ask your partners a question, and then they answer it.

Step 3. Find the Feeling Stickers for their answers.

Step 4. Attach the stickers to the frame.

WRITING

G Listen, circle, and write. **14**

```
angry        hungry        sleepy        thirsty
```

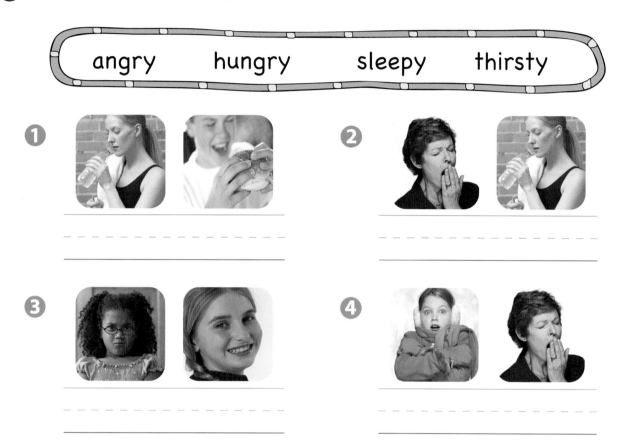

1 _____

2 _____

3 _____

4 _____

H Read, look, and complete the sentences.

1 Q Are you — — — — — — — — — — ?

A Yes, — — — — — — — — — — .

cold

2 Q — — — — — — — — — — angry?

A No, she isn't. She's — — — — — — — .

happy

PHONICS LISTENING ⑮

I Listen and read the phonics story.

Lawn! In the lawn!

Paul saw a fawn.

He gives it a few apples.

Shawn saw a hawk.

He gives it some raw meat.

Are you scared?

No, we're not.

We're having fun.

J Listen and circle the correct diphthongs. Then write the right words.

| lawn | paul | raw | fawn | few | hawk |

1. (au **|** aw) _____

2. (au **|** ew) _____

3. (au **|** aw) _____

4. (au **|** aw) _____

5. (aw **|** ew) _____

6. (ew **|** aw) _____

UNIT 04

There Is Some Salt

A Listen and chant.
Then circle the food you hear in the chant.

B Listen, circle, and match.

1  ○   ○ sugar

2  ○   ○ ketchup

3  ○   ○ butter

4  ○   ○ cereal

C Listen, check, and circle the word.

1

honey ▮ ketchup

2

cheese ▮ cereal

3

salt ▮ pepper

4

pepper ▮ butter

D Listen, check, and match.

1

SUGAR | HONEY

•   • Is there any cheese?

2

SUGAR | BUTTER

•   • Is there any honey?

3

cheese | KETCHUP

•   • Is there any salt?

4

cereal | SALT

•   • Is there any sugar?

E Listen, look, and circle "a" or "b".

1  a / b

2  a / b

3  a / b

4  a / b

5  a / b

6  a / b

SPEAK & PLAY

F Ask and answer with your partner. Follow the steps below.

Is there any _____?

Yes, there is. There is some _____. /
No, there isn't. There isn't any _____.

sugar	ketchup	butter
cereal	salt	pepper
cheese	honey	

Step 1. Find a partner.

Step 2. Choose some Food Stickers, and then attach the stickers to the table.

Step 3. Your partner asks you a question, and then you answer it.

WRITING

G Listen, circle, and write. 🔵19

butter   cheese   ketchup   pepper

1   SALT

2

3   SUGAR

4   SALT

H Read, look, and complete the sentences using "some" or "any".

1 **Q** Is there _____ ?

   A Yes, there is. There is _____ .

cereal

2 **Q** Is there _____ butter?

   A No, there isn't. There isn't _____ .

honey

I Listen and read the phonics story.

Open the door!
Foot in the pool!
Look at the moon!
A cool wind blows.

Are there any shooting stars?
Yes, there are.
There are some stars.

J Listen and circle the correct diphthongs. Then write the right words.

door   foot   pool   look   moon   shooting

1. (long oo | short oo) _____   **2.** (long oo | short oo) _____

3. (long oo | short oo) _____   **4.** (long oo | short oo) _____

5. (long oo | short oo) _____   **6.** (long oo | short oo) _____

UNIT 05

I Want to Be a Teacher

CHANT LISTENING 21

A Listen and chant.
Then circle the occupations you hear in the chant.

B Listen, write the number, and match.

farmer   pilot   police officer   doctor

C Listen, look, and circle.

1

    police officer   firefighter   teacher

2

    farmer   teacher   pilot

3

    nurse   doctor   artist

4

    nurse   farmer   doctor

SENTENCE LISTENING 23

D Listen, check, and match.

1.
   - I want to be an artist.

2.
   - I want to be a doctor.

3.
   - I want to be a police officer.

4.
   - I want to be a pilot.

E Listen, look, and circle "a" or "b".

1. a / b
2. a / b
3. a / b
4. a / b
5. a / b
6. a / b

SPEAK & PLAY

F Ask and answer with your partner. Follow the steps below.

What do you want to be?

I want to be a/an _____.

doctor	teacher	nurse
pilot	farmer	artist
police officer	firefighter	

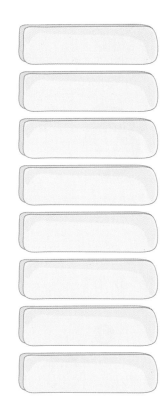

Step 1. Find eight partners.

Step 2. You ask your partners a question, and then they answer it.

Step 3. Find the Word Sticker for their answer.

Step 4. Attach the sticker in a box, and then connect the word and the right picture.

WRITING

G Listen, circle, and write. **24**

nurse   farmer   firefighter   police officer

①

_____

②

_____

③

_____

④

_____

H Read, look, and complete the sentences using "a" or "an".

① **Q** What do you want to be?

A I want to be _____ .

doctor

② **Q** What do you want to be?

A I want to be _____ .

artist

I Listen and read the phonics story.

I can make cheesecake and cherry pie.
I can cook fried shrimp and chicken.
I can make a shellfish dish.

What do you want to be?
I want to be a chef.

Chris wants to be a chef.

J Listen and circle the correct consonant diphthongs. Then write the right words.

cheese cherry shrimp chicken shell chef

1. (ch | sh) _____

2. (ch | sh) _____

3. (ch | sh) _____

4. (ch | sh) _____

5. (ch | sh) _____

6. (ch | sh) _____

Listen and write the letter "a", "b", or "c". 26

1
  and the sock image

2
firefighter, woman,  1st

3

4

 Listen, unscramble the word, and match. 27

1 nayrg   →   a_____ ○   ○

2 vesolg   →   g_____ ○   ○

3 chupket → k_____ ○   ○

4 dnocse → s_____ ○   ○

C Listen and match. 28

1  What grade are you in? ○ — ○ Yes, he is.

2 Is he sad? ○ — ○ I want to be a police officer.

3 What do you want to be? ○ — ○ Yes, there is. There is some salt.

4 What are those? ○ — ○ I'm in the second grade.

5  Is there any salt? ○ — ○ Those are socks.

D Listen, find the picture, and write the number. 29

E Listen, write the number, and match. **30**

[ ] What does she want to be? ○ ○ No, there isn't.

[ ] What are those? ○ ○ She wants to be a nurse.

[ ] Is he a pilot? ○ ○ Yes, he is.

[ ] Is there any pepper? ○ ○ Those are socks and shoes.

F Listen, look, and complete the sentences. **31**

any be fifth grade police officer some

❶

5th

Q What _____ are you in?

A I am in the _____ grade.

❷

Q What do you want to _____?

A I want to be a _____.

❸

Q Is there _____ honey?

A Yes, there is. There is _____ honey.

G Listen to the words and circle them. 32

1 four | flow   2 joy | toy   3 sew | sauce
4 hoop | hook   5 cheek | shake   6 owl | oil
7 paw | dow   8 witch | wash   9 push | watch

H Listen, check, and write the words. 33

1
_____

2
_____

3
_____

4
_____

I Listen and circle the correct diphthongs. Then write the right words. 34

1. (oi | ou) _____   2. (long oo | short oo) _____
3. (aw | ew) _____   4. (ch | sh) _____
5. (ou | ow) _____   6. (oy | au) _____
7. (au | ou) _____   8. (oi | oy) _____
9. (short oo | long oo) _____   10. (sh | ch) _____
11. (au | aw) _____   12. (ow | ew) _____

He Rides a Bike

CHANT LISTENING 35

A Listen and chant.
Then circle the activities you hear in the chant.

WORD LISTENING 🔟

B Listen, circle, and match.

1.
2.
3.
4.

takes a shower

does homework

watches TV

eats snacks

C Listen, check, and circle the word.

1.
practices the piano
takes a shower

2.
rides a bike
eats snacks

3.
does homework
plays computer games

4.
cleans her room
practices the piano

SENTENCE LISTENING 🔟37

D Listen, check, and match.

1
- She takes a shower.

2
- He does his homework.

3
- He eats snacks.

4
- She cleans her room.

E Listen, look, and circle "a" or "b".

1  a / b

2  a / b

3  a / b

4  a / b

5  a / b

6  a / b

SPEAK & PLAY

F Ask and answer with your partner. Follow the steps below.

What does he/she do after school?

He/She _____.

rides a bike
does his/her homework
watches TV
eats snacks
practices the piano
takes a shower
plays computer games
cleans his/her room

START~!

FINISH!

Step 1. Find a partner.

Step 2. Your partner asks you a question, and then you look at the picture in order and answer it.

Step 3. Find the Word Sticker for your answer.

Step 4. Attach the sticker below the picture.

WRITING

Listen, circle, and write. 38

does homework   practices the piano   rides a bike   watches TV

1

_____

2

_____

3

_____

4

_____

H Read, look, and complete the sentences using "He" or "She".

1 Q What does he do after school?

   A _____ .

takes a shower

2 Q What does she do after school?

   A _____ .

cleans her room

Consonant Diphthongs **ph, wh**

I Listen and read the phonics story.

Who is Philip?

He is a boy.

Where is Philip's house?

It's on White Street.

What is his phone number?

It's 976-1042.

What does Philip do after school?

He takes photos.

J Listen and circle the correct consonant diphthongs. Then write the right words.

who   Philip   white   what   phone   photo

1. (ph **|** wh) _____

2. (ph **|** wh) _____

3. (wh **|** ph) _____

4. (wh **|** ph) _____

5. (ph **|** wh) _____

6. (ph **|** wh) _____

UNIT 07
I Go There by Bus

A Listen and chant.
Then circle the kinds of transportation you hear in the chant.

WORD LISTENING 41

B Listen, write the number, and match.

ferry   airplane   train   subway

C Listen, look, and circle.

①    airplane   bus   car

②    ferry   helicopter   train

③    taxi   airplane   ferry

④    car   ferry   bus

D Listen, check, and match.

1 ○   ○ I go there by train.

2 ○   ○ I go there by airplane.

3 ○   ○ I go there by ferry.

4 ○   ○ I go there by taxi.

E Listen, look, and circle "a" or "b".

1  a / b

2  a / b

3  a / b

4  a / b

5  a / b

6  a / b

SPEAK & PLAY

F Ask and answer with your partner. Follow the steps below.

How do you go there?

I go there by _____.

bus   taxi   car   train
ferry   airplane
helicopter   subway

taxi   car

bus   train

subway   ferry

helicopter   airplane

Step 1. Find a partner.

Step 2. Your partner asks you a question pointing a transportation, and then you answer it.

Step 3. Find the Transportation Sticker for your answer.

Step 4. Attach the sticker on the dart board.

WRITING

G Listen, circle, and write. **43**

airplane   ferry   helicopter   subway

1

_____
- - - - - - - - - - - - - -
_____

2

_____
- - - - - - - - - - - - - -
_____

3

_____
- - - - - - - - - - - - - -
_____

4

_____
- - - - - - - - - - - - - -
_____

H Read, look, and complete the sentences using "by".

1 Q How do you go there?

_____
A I go there - - - - - - - - - - - - - - - .
_____

taxi

2 Q How does he go there?

_____
A He goes there - - - - - - - - - - - - - - - .
_____

bus

Consonant Diphthongs | **voiceless th, voiced th**

I Listen and read the phonics story.

Weather! The weather is great!
Heather has a feather bag.
My brother has three balls.
My father reads a thick book.
My mother reads a thin book.

How do they go to the park?
They go there by bus.

J Listen and circle the correct consonant diphthongs. Then write the right words.

weather   heather   feather   three   thick   thin

1. (voiceless th **|** voiced th) _____   **2.** (voiceless th **|** voiced th) _____

3. (voiceless th **|** voiced th) _____   **4.** (voiceless th **|** voiced th) _____

5. (voiceless th **|** voiced th) _____   **6.** (voiceless th **|** voiced th) _____

It's Mine

CHANT LISTENING 45

A Listen and chant.
Then circle the things you hear in the chant.

WORD LISTENING 🔊

B Listen, circle, and match.

1

2

3

4

- comb
- umbrella
- watch
- camera

C Listen, check, and circle the word.

1
toothbrush | camera

2
key | comb

3
wallet | watch

4
umbrella | backpack

D Listen, check, and match.

1.   ○   ○ Is this my toothbrush?

2.   ○   ○ Is this her umbrella?

3.   ○   ○ Is this your backpack?

4.   ○   ○ Is this his wallet?

E Listen, look, and circle "a" or "b".

1. a b
2. a b
3. a b
4. a b
5. a b
6. a b

SPEAK & PLAY

F Ask and answer with your partner. Follow the steps below.

Is this my/your/her/his _____?

Yes, it is.
It's yours/mine/hers/his.

umbrella	key	watch
backpack	wallet	camera
toothbrush	comb	

I	You	He	She

Step 1. Find a partner.

Step 2. Your partner asks you a question, and then you answer it.

Step 3. Find the Word and Picture Sticker for your answer.

Step 4. Attach the sticker on the chart.

WRITING

G Listen, circle, and write. **48**

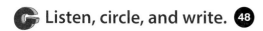

| wallet | backpack | umbrella | toothbrush |

1

_____

2

_____

3

_____

4

_____

H Read, look, and complete the sentences using "It's".

1 **Q** Is this your _____ ?

A Yes, it is. _____ .

key

2 **Q** Is this her _____ ?

A Yes, it is. _____ .

comb

I Listen and read the phonics story.

Happy turns off the light.
Puppy has puffy hair.
Hippo has floppy hair.
They are Miffy and Hoppy.

Are these your pets?
Yes, they are. They're mine.

J Listen and write the correct double letters and a word.

puffy happy puppy hippo floppy slipper

1. ha ➕ _____ ➕ y ➖ _____
2. sli ➕ _____ ➕ er ➖ _____
3. pu ➕ _____ ➕ y ➖ _____
4. hi ➕ _____ ➕ o ➖ _____
5. flo ➕ _____ ➕ y ➖ _____
6. pu ➕ _____ ➕ y ➖ _____

UNIT 09
I Was at the Bakery

CHANT LISTENING 50

A Listen and chant.
Then circle the places you hear in the chant.

B Listen, write the number, and match.

○   ○   ○   ○

(gym)   (movie theater)   (beauty salon)   (amusement park)

C Listen, look, and circle.

1    drugstore   bookstore   movie theater

2    restaurant   bakery   gym

3    beauty salon   bookstore   amusement park

4    movie theater   drugstore   bakery

SENTENCE LISTENING ⑤

D Listen, check, and match.

1 ○   ○ I was at the bakery.

2 ○   ○ I was at the movie theater.

3 ○   ○ I was at the gym.

4 ○   ○ I was at the restaurant.

E Listen, look, and circle "a" or "b".

1  a / b

2  a / b

3  a / b

4  a / b

5  a / b

6  a / b

SPEAK & PLAY

F Ask and answer with your partner. Follow the steps below.

Where were you?

I was at the _____.

bakery	drugstore
amusement park	bookstore
gym	restaurant
beauty salon	movie theater

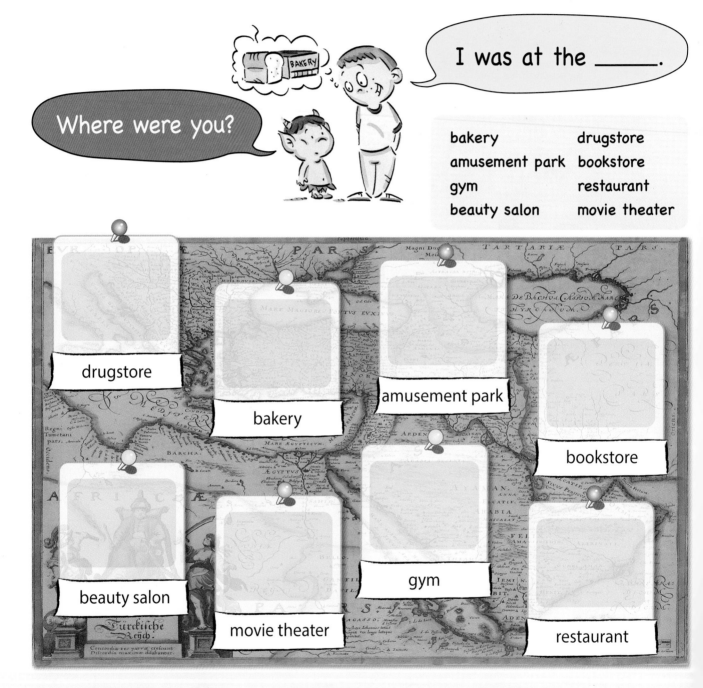

drugstore

bakery

amusement park

bookstore

beauty salon

movie theater

gym

restaurant

Step 1. Find a partner.

Step 2. Your partner asks you a question, and then you answer it.

Step 3. Find the Picture Sticker for your answer.

Step 4. Attach the sticker above the word.

WRITING

G Listen, circle, and write. 53

amusement park   beauty salon   movie theater   restaurant

❶

_____

_____

❷

_____

_____

❸

_____

_____

❹

_____

_____

H Read, look, and complete the sentences using "at the".

❶ **Q** Where were you?

A I was _____ .

gym

❷ **Q** Where was he?

A He was _____ .

drugstore

Double Letters **bb, dd**

I Listen and read the phonics story.

Bobby looks for his buddy.

His buddy is Todd.

There! There is Todd.

Where were you, Todd?

I was in the pool.

I paddled.

I made bubbles.

J Listen and circle the correct double letters. Then write the right words.

buddy   bubble   paddle   middle

1. (bb | dd) _____

2. (bb | dd) _____

3. (bb | dd) _____

4. (bb | dd) _____

UNIT 10

I Played Chess

CHANT LISTENING 55

A Listen and chant.
Then circle the activities you hear in the chant.

WORD LISTENING 56

B Listen, circle, and match.

1.  ○   ○ walked the dog

2.  ○   ○ had a party

3.  ○   ○ went shopping

4. ○   ○ made a cake

C Listen, check, and circle the word.

1.
studied math | played chess

2.
saw a movie | made a cake

3.
walked the dog | played chess

4.
had a party | watched TV

SENTENCE LISTENING 57

D Listen, check, and match.

1

• • I had a party.

2

• • I saw a movie.

3

• • I went shopping.

4

• • I made a cake.

E Listen, look, and circle "a" or "b".

1  a / b

2  a / b

3  a / b

4  a / b

5  a / b

6  a / b

SPEAK & PLAY

F Ask and answer with your partner. Follow the steps below.

What did you do yesterday?

I _____.

watched TV	played chess
studied math	walked the dog
went shopping	saw a movie
made a cake	had a party

Step 1. Find eight partners and write their names in the blanks.

Step 2. You ask your partner a question, and then he/she answers it.

Step 3. Find the Picture Sticker for the answer.

Step 4. Attach the sticker below the name.

WRITING

 Listen, circle, and write. 58

had a party   saw a movie   studied math   went shopping

1

_____

_____

2

_____

_____

3

_____

_____

4

_____

_____

H Read, look, and complete the sentences.

1 Q What did you do yesterday?

A I _____.

made a cake

2 Q What did you do yesterday?

A I _____.

walked the dog

Double Letters **ll, rr**

I Listen and read the phonics story.

Many balloons.
Grilled turkey.
Strawberry jelly.
A tall Christmas tree.

Merry Christmas, Kerry!
What did you do yesterday?
I went to the mall.
I bought these things.

J Listen and write the correct double letters and a word.

> balloon   grill   strawberry   jelly   tall   merry

1. gri ⊕ _____ ⊖ _____
2. ba ⊕ _____ ⊕ oon ⊖ _____
3. ta ⊕ _____ ⊖ _____
4. me ⊕ _____ ⊕ y ⊖ _____
5. strawbe ⊕ _____ ⊕ y ⊖ _____
6. je ⊕ _____ ⊕ y ⊖ _____

REVIEW 2　Units 6~10

A Listen and write the letter "a", "b", or "c". 60

①

②

③

④

B Listen, unscramble the words, and match. 61

① nealpair → a_____ ○

② bomc → c_____ ○

③ stretauran → r_____ ○

④ yrrfe → f_____ ○

C Listen and match. **62**

1  How do you go there? ○   ○ I walked the dog.

2 What does he do after school? ○   ○ He rides a bike.

3 What did you do yesterday? ○   ○ I go there by airplane.

4  Is this your umbrella? ○   ○ I was at the bakery.

5  Where were you? ○   ○ Yes, it is. It's mine.

D Listen, find the picture, and write the number. **63**

E Listen, write the number, and match. 🔵64

☐ Is this our car? ⚬	⚬ I went there by taxi.
☐ Where were they? ⚬	⚬ Yes, it is. It's ours.
☐ How did you go there? ⚬	⚬ They were at the gym.
☐ What did he do? ⚬	⚬ He practiced the piano.

F Listen, look, and complete the sentences. 🔵65

bus   camera   do   go   plays   theirs   went

1

Q What does he _____ after school?

A He _____ computer games.

2

Q How did you _____ there?

A I _____ there by _____.

3

Q Is this their _____?

A Yes, it is. It's _____.

PHONICS REVIEW

G Listen to the words and circle them. **66**

① why **|** phone   ② thin **|** thick   ③ puff **|** puppy

④ buddy **|** bubble   ⑤ Jerry **|** jelly   ⑥ father **|** feather

⑦ coffee **|** hippo   ⑧ Todd **|** buddy   ⑨ worry **|** Kerry

H Listen, check, and write the words. **67**

①

_____

②

_____

③

_____

④

_____

I Listen and circle the correct letters. Then write the right words. **68**

1. (voiced th **|** voiceless th) _____   2. (ph **|** ff) _____

3. (wh **|** voiceless th) _____   4. (rr **|** ll) _____

5. (dd **|** bb) _____   6. (voiceless th **|** dd) _____

7. (pp **|** ff) _____   8. (bb **|** ph) _____

9. (ll **|** rr) _____   10. (voiced th **|** ff) _____

11. (bb **|** dd) _____   12. (wh **|** ph) _____

CHANT LIST

What are these? What are these?

These are socks. Socks, socks.

These are gloves. Gloves, gloves.

What are these? What are these?

These are shoes. Shoes, shoes.

These are pants. Pants, pants.

What are those? What are those?

Those are shirts. Shirts, shirts.

Those are skirts. Skirts, skirts.

What are those? What are those?

Those are jackets. Jackets, jackets.

Those are hats. Hats, hats.

What grade are you in?

First grade. I'm in the first grade.

What grade are you in?

Second grade. I'm in the second grade.

What grade are you in?

Third grade. I'm in the third grade.

What grade are you in?

Fourth grade. I'm in the fourth grade.

First, second, third, fourth.

What grade are you in?

Fifth grade. I'm in the fifth grade.

What grade are you in?

Sixth grade. I'm in the sixth grade.

What grade are you in?

Seventh grade. I'm in the seventh grade.

What grade are you in?

Eighth grade. I'm in the eighth grade.

Fifth, sixth, seventh, eighth.

Are you happy? Yes, I am. I'm happy.

Are you sad? Yes, I am. I'm sad.

Is he hot? Yes, he is. He's hot.

Is she cold? Yes, she is. She's cold.

Are you angry? Yes, I am. I'm angry.

Are you sleepy? Yes, I am. I'm sleepy.

Is he hungry? Yes, he is. He's hungry.

Is he thirsty? Yes, he is. He's thirsty.

Is there any salt? Yes, there is. There is some salt.

Is there any sugar? Yes, there is. There is some sugar.

Is there any pepper? Yes, there is. There is some pepper.

Is there any ketchup? Yes, there is. There is some ketchup.

Is there any butter? No, there isn't. There isn't any butter.

Is there any cheese? No, there isn't. There isn't any cheese.

Is there any honey? No, there isn't. There isn't any honey.

Is there any water? No, there isn't. There isn't any water.

What do you want to be?

A teacher, a teacher. I want to be a teacher.

A doctor, a doctor. I want to be a doctor.

What do you want to be?

A police officer, a police officer.

I want to be a police officer.

A firefighter, a firefighter. I want to be a firefighter.

What do you want to be?

A nurse, a nurse. I want to be a nurse.

A farmer, a farmer. I want to be a farmer.

What do you want to be?

A pilot, a pilot. I want to be a pilot.

An artist, an artist. I want to be an artist.

Unit 6 He Rides a Bike

Page 41

What does he do? What does he do after school?
He rides a bike. He eats snacks.
What does he do? What does he do after school?
He watches TV. He does his homework.

What does she do? What does she do after school?
She cleans her room. She practices the piano.
What does she do? What does she do after school?
She takes a shower. She plays computer games.

Unit 7 I Go There by Bus

Page 47

How, how? How do you go there?
Bus, bus. I go there by bus.
Taxi, taxi. I go there by taxi.
How, how? How do you go there?
Car, car. I go there by car.
Train, train. I go there by train.

How, how? How does he go there?
Subway, subway. He goes there by subway.
Helicopter, helicopter. He goes there by helicopter.
How, how? How does she go there?
Airplane, airplane. She goes there by airplane.
Ferry, ferry. She goes there by ferry.

Is this your umbrella? Yes, it is. It's mine.

Is this my key? Yes, it is. It's yours.

Is this his watch? Yes, it is. It's his.

Is this her backpack? Yes, it is. It's hers.

My, mine, you, yours, his, his, her, hers.

Is this your wallet? Yes, it is. It's mine.

Is this my camera? Yes, it is. It's yours.

Is this his toothbrush? Yes, it is. It's his.

Is this her comb? Yes, it is. It's hers.

My, mine, you, yours, his, his, her, hers.

Where were you? Where were you?

Bakery, bakery. I was at the bakery.

Drugstore, drugstore. I was at the drugstore.

Where were you? Where were you?

Amusement park, amusement park. I was at the amusement park.

Movie theater, movie theater. I was at the movie theater.

Where was he? Where was he?

Bookstore, bookstore. He was at the bookstore.

Restaurant, restaurant. He was at the restaurant.

Where was she? Where was she?

Gym, gym. She was at the gym.

Beauty salon, beauty salon. She was at the beauty salon.

What did you do yesterday?
I played chess. I played chess.
I watched TV. I watched TV.
What did you do yesterday?
I studied math. I studied math.
I walked the dog. I walked the dog.

What did you do yesterday?
I went shopping. I went shopping.
I saw a movie. I saw a movie.
What did you do yesterday?
I made a cake. I made a cake.
I had a party. I had a party.

p.10

p.16

first	second	third	fourth
fifth	sixth	seventh	eighth

p.22

p.28

HONEY   SUGAR   BUTTER   SALT   PEPPER   KETCHUP

p.34

doctor	nurse	farmer	artist
teacher	pilot	police officer	firefighter

p.44

rides a bike	does his/her homework	watches TV	eats snacks
practices the piano	takes a shower	plays computer games	cleans his/her room

p.50

p.56

mine
yours
his
hers

p.62

p.68